Note For Parents

In addition to the many fun activities in this book—mazes, join-the-dots, spot the differences and colouring pages—*More Unicorn Best Friends Forever Activity Book* also includes thinking prompts. The open-ended questions in these prompts are designed to help children express themselves and think creatively. These can be used as conversation starters. Discuss the questions with your child or ask them to write their responses in a notebook, or do both. The emphasis should be on thinking rather than just writing. We hope your child enjoys their time with unicorns and you in this magical book.

Published by Red Panda, an imprint of Westland Books, a division of Nasadiya Technologies Private Limited, in 2025

No. 269/2B, First Floor, 'Irai Arul', Vimalraj Street, Nethaji Nagar, Alapakkam Main Road, Maduravoyal, Chennai 600095

Westland, the Westland logo, Red Panda and the Red Panda logo are the trademarks of Nasadiya Technologies Private Limited, or its affiliates.

Copyright © Nasadiya Technologies Private Limited, 2025

ISBN: 9789371975506

10 9 8 7 6 5 4 3 2 1

All rights reserved

Images sourced from Shutterstock

Printed at Nutech Print Services Pvt. Ltd

No part of this book may be reproduced, or stored in a retrieval system, or transmitted in any form or by any means, electronic, mechanical, photocopying, recording, or otherwise, without express written permission of the publisher.

Join the dots to reveal the secret picture of the unicorn.

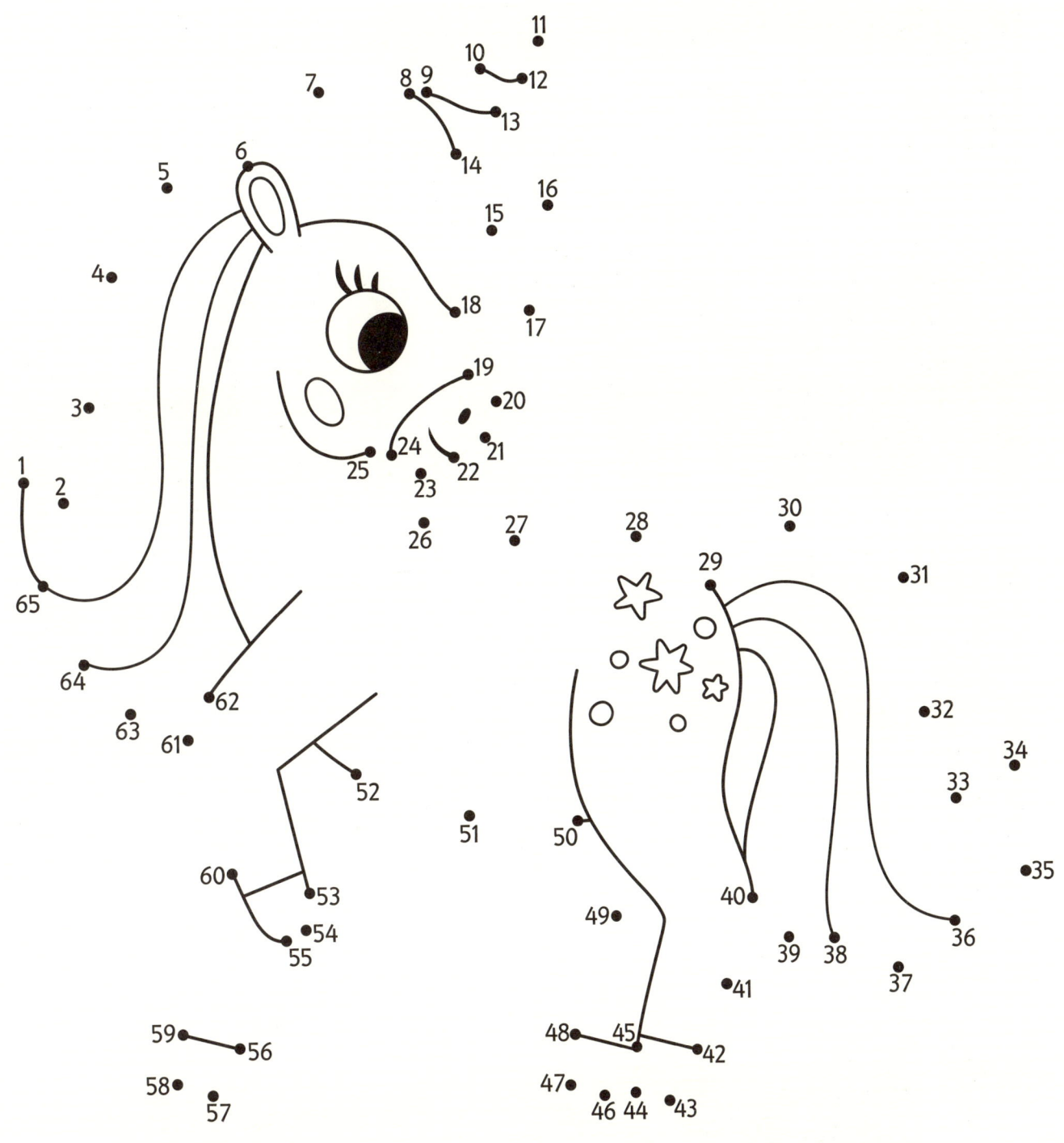

What would you name this unicorn pookie?

Can you spot all 10 mermaids hiding in this picture?

Shh ... Baby unicorn is sleeping. But there seems to be a piece missing. Can you find the missing piece?

What do unicorns do all day? Match the fun things they do with the right picture!

7:00 AM
Unicorn brushes her sparkly teeth.

8:00 AM
Unicorn nibbles her breakfast with a chomp.

11:00 AM
Unicorn reads her twinkly rainbow book.

4:00 PM
Unicorn giggles and plays with her friends.

9:00 PM
Unicorn snuggles into her cozy bed and snoozes off.

What does your day look like? Describe your 'Day in my life.'

Colour the unicorn's world by numbers! Watch the magic appear as you fill in each number.

Oh no! Magic Dust's magical pattern is not finished. Can you guess what comes next?

Roselet and Moon Wings are enjoying their favourite milkshakes! Use the magic key below to decode their flavours and write them in the space provided.

CHOCOLATE

STRAWBERRY

Magic Key

O B H A Y S L E R W C T

Match the unicorns with their shadows by drawing a line.

Look at your shadow. What does it remind you of? Talk about what you notice and how it makes you feel. Can you tell a story about your shadow?

Match each picture with its perfect pair!

Look closely! Can you spot 10 magical differences between the two pictures.

Roselet is counting the items in her treasure box. Can you help her by circling the correct number?

6 5 7   7 8 9

5 7 6   5 6 4

If you had a treasure box, what would you keep inside? Draw or write about your special treasures and why they are important to you.

Every unicorn's horn is special. The swirls on the horn holds magical powers! Use the legend below to choose any four powers for your unicorn. Decorate each swirl of the horn with the matching pattern.

Star: Makes the night sky twinkle brighter and calls friendly fireflies.

Heart: Spreads kindness so everyone feels warm and caring.

Lightning: Gives super-speed, faster than the wind!

Raindrop: Brings gentle showers to help flowers grow.

Swirl: Creates rainbows wherever the unicorn gallops.

Diamond: Protects with a sparkling shield that keeps friends safe.

Colour this baby unicorn as she glides through the stars.

Can you count all the sparkly stars around the baby unicorn?

Help the unicorn climb the right ladders and trace the path to her fluffy cloud home!

The unicorn is is leaping through the stars. Join the dots in order to see him appear.

Look at the unicorn party pictures and spot 10 differences between them.

Do you like having parties with your friends? Think about your perfect party and share all the fun things you would do together.

Solve these magical sums to help Emily Isabelle unlock her treasures.

 = 2  = 3  = 7  = 9

 −  +  = ☐

 +  −  = ☐

 −  +  = ☐

 −  +  = ☐

The unicorn is having a party and singing her favourite song. Colour her to join the fun.

What's your favourite song? Sing it out loud and think about why you love it.

The unicorns are having fun with their friends! Can you count how many birds, butterflies, unicorns and hearts you see? Write the number in the boxes below each picture.

Unicorn Land is full of surprises today! Can you spot 10 things that looks odd?

Look at the two pictures of the fairy princess in the garden and spot 5 differences.

Look at all the unicorns and circle the two identical unicorns..

The unicorns lost their gifts in the twisty maze! Can you trace the path through the maze to find it before it disappears?

Oh oh! Half of the rainbow has vanished. Help Rainbow Cookie draw the missing half and colouring it in.

Find and trace the odd one out in each line

Welcome to Sparkle's pastry shop! Some cakes are missing from the shelf. Can you match the cakes to their shadows?

Use the colour code to finish the picture.

The unicorns are dancing at their grand party. But there's a mushroom hiding among them! Can you find it?

Follow the unicorns in the correct order.

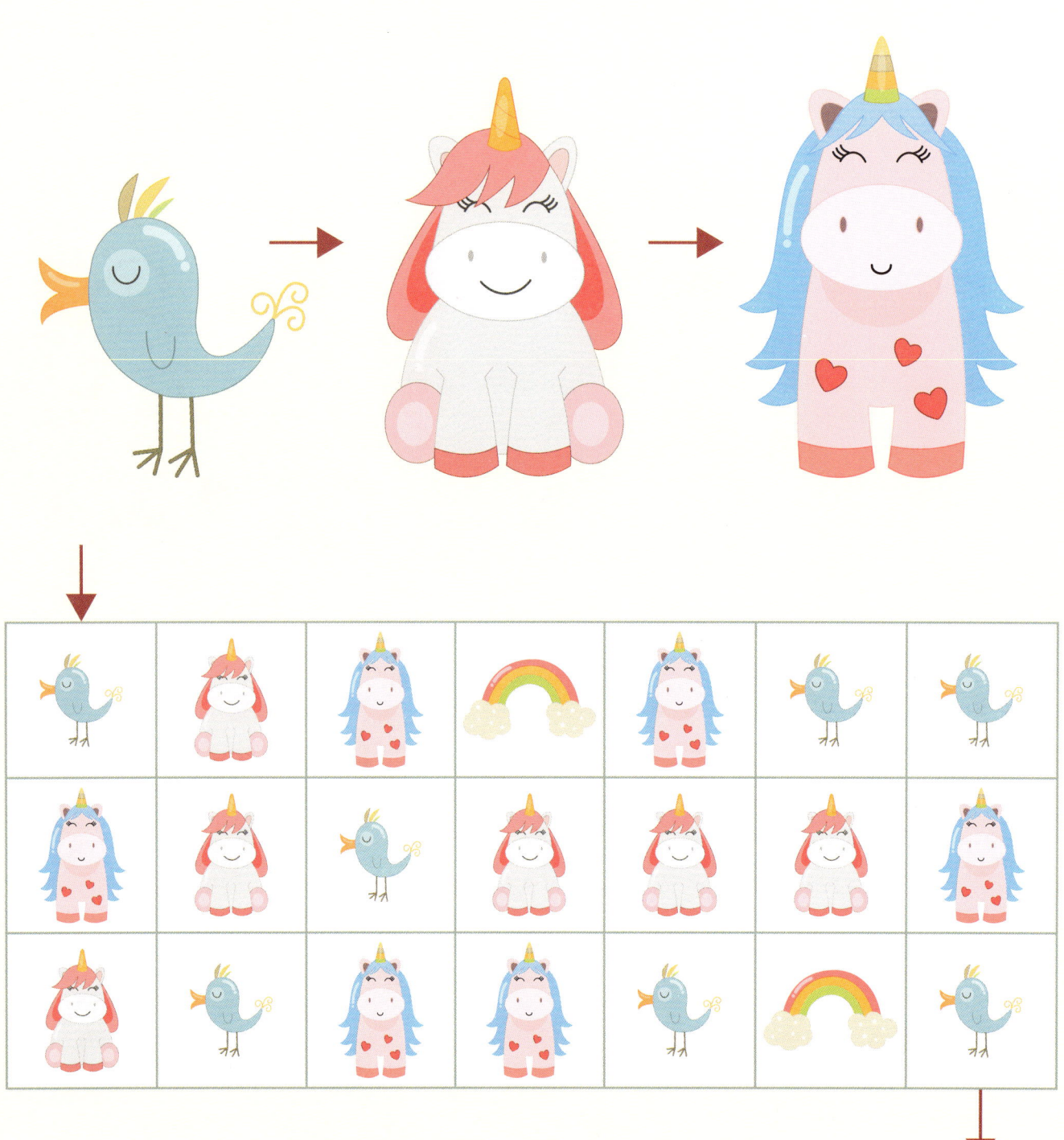

Follow the blue crystals to help the princess and her unicorn get to the castle.

Help Magic Dust circle the odd thing that doesn't belong in each line!

  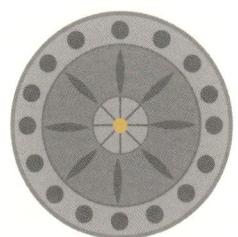 

To see what the princess whispers to the unicorn, hold this page up to a mirror and peek!

YOU ARE MY
LUCKY CHARM

The unicorn is having fun in the rain. Can you colour her to brighten up her day?

Write the missing numbers correctly to complete the unicorns' mission.

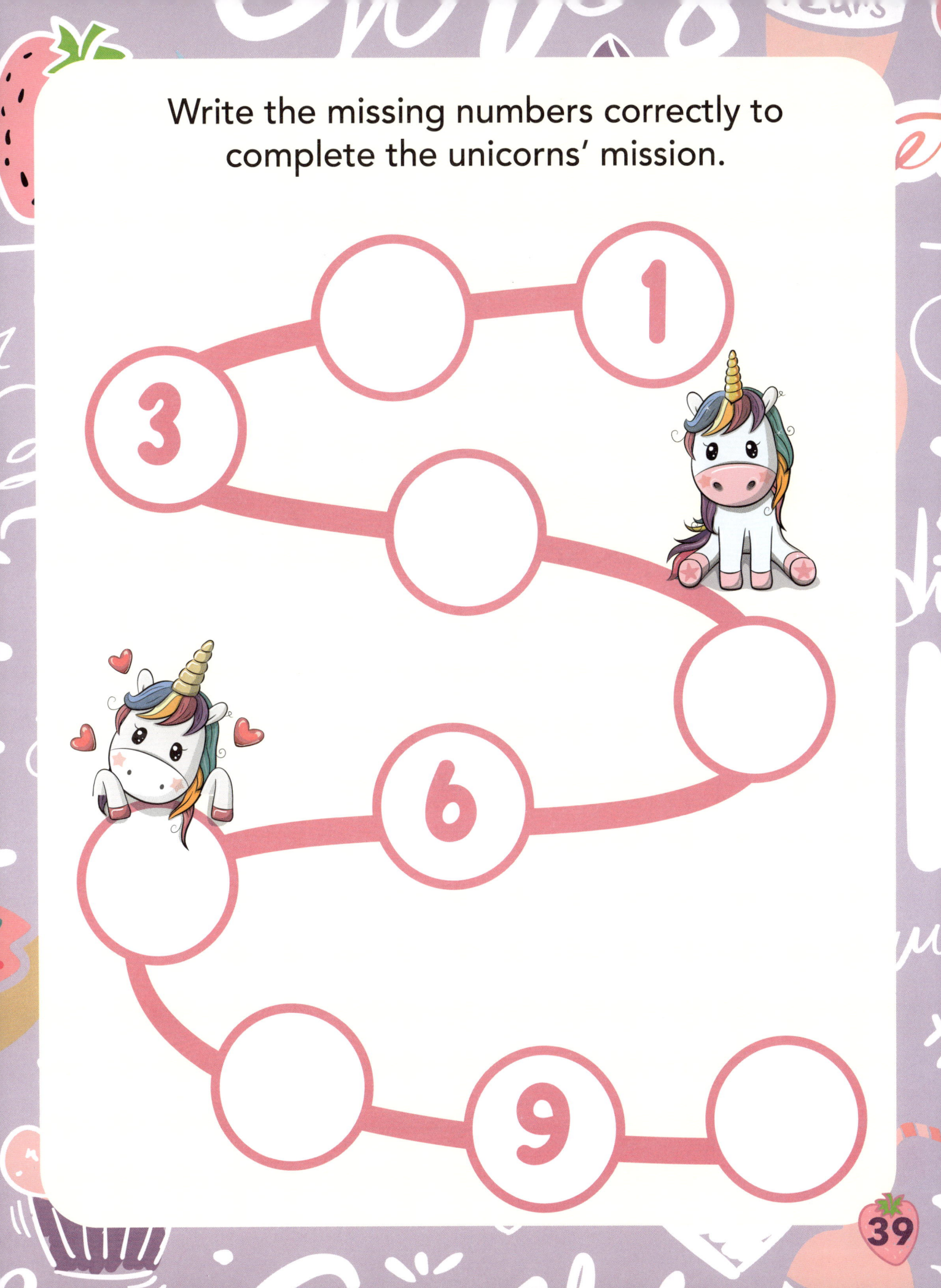

Connect the enchanted dots in numerical order from 1 to 90, to magically reveal the secret picture!

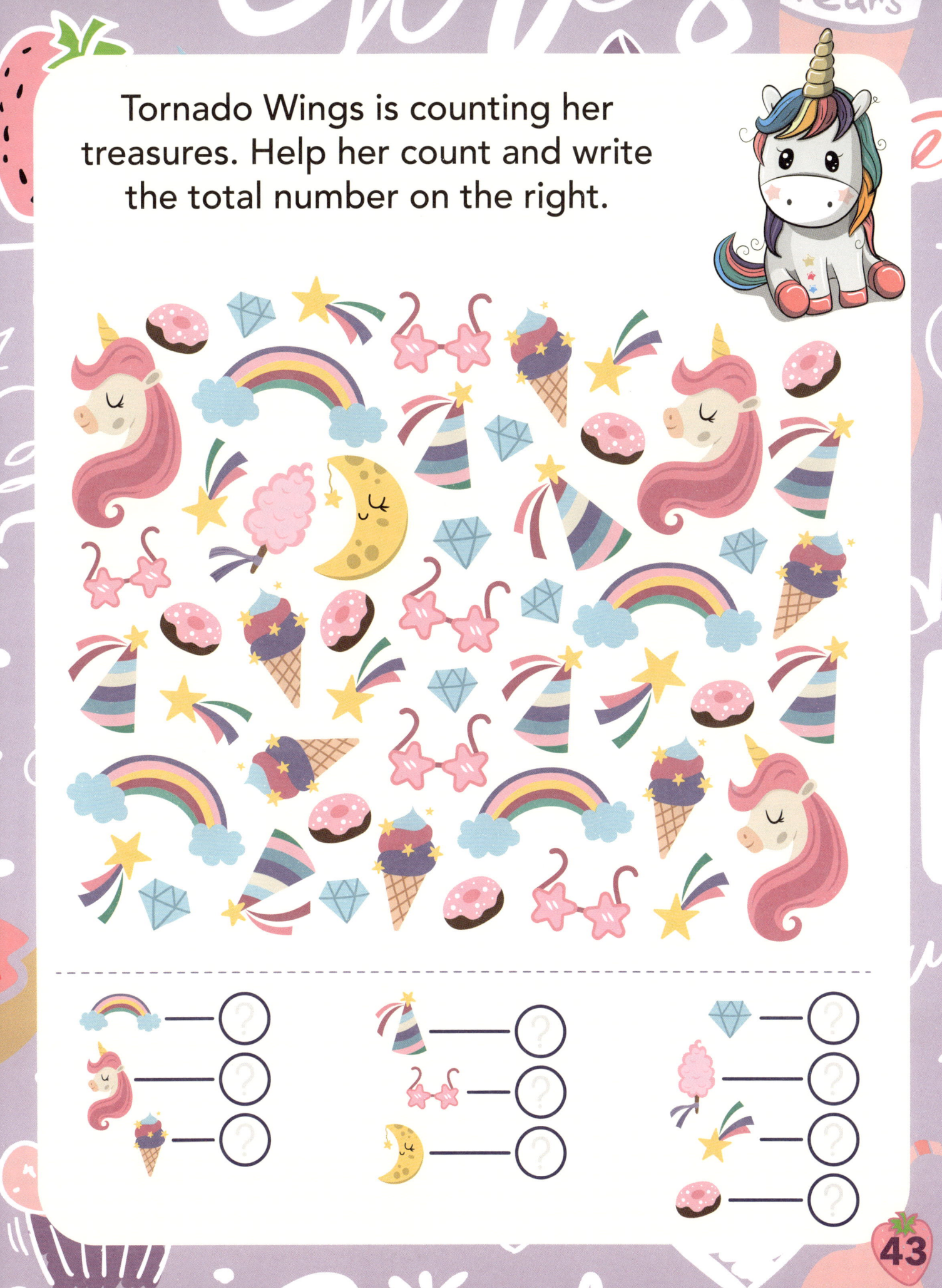

Tornado Wings is counting her treasures. Help her count and write the total number on the right.

What comes next?

The unicorns are playing hide-and-seek in this magical land! Can you help each unicorn find its spot? Pick the matching unicorn sticker from the last page and place it in the right place.

Page 4:

Page 6:

Page 7:

Page 8:

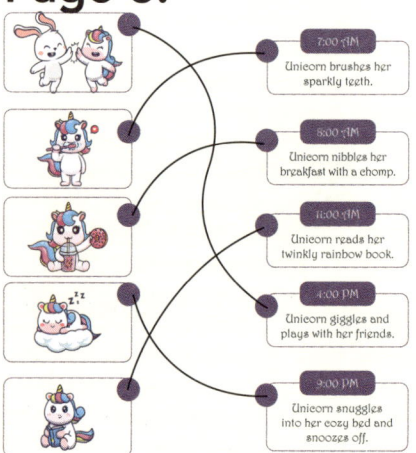

Page 10:

Page 11: Chocolate Strawberry

Page 13:

Page 14:

page 15: 7 Dimonds; 8 Bows; 6 Cupcakes; 5 Crowns

Page 18:

Page 20:

Page 21: 10; 6; 14; 8

Page 23:

Page 24:

page 26:

Page 28:

page 30:

page 31:

Page 33

Page 34:

page 35:

Page 36:

Page 37: YOU ARE MY LUCKY CHARM

Page 41:

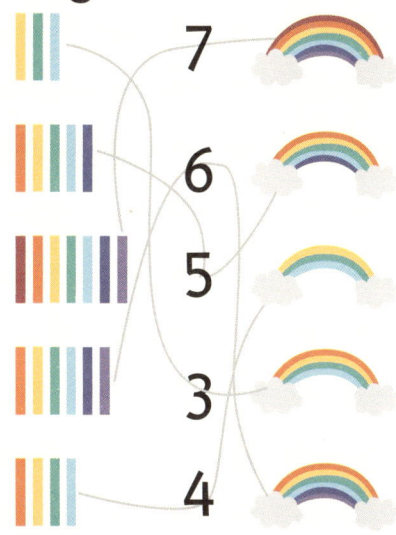

Page 42:

Page 43:

Page 44

Cover:
10 dimonds and 8 butterflies

The red panda is a reddish-brown mammal with a long, ringed tail and a raccoon-like face. Also called a firefox, it is found in the forest of the eastern Himalayas. In India, it lives in Sikkim, Arunachal Pradesh, in the Darjeeling district of West Bengal, and parts of Meghalaya. Its diet includes bamboo shoots and leaves, grass, fruit, roots and insects. The cat-sized red panda uses its bushy tail for balance and to wrap around its body for warmth up in the mountains. The red panda is now an endangered species, with less than 10,000 left in the wild.